Wakeboarding
Techniques and Tricks

Stephanie Cooperman

the rosen publishing group's
rosen central

Published in 2003 by The Rosen Publishing Group, Inc.
29 East 21st Street, New York, NY 10010

First Edition

Library of Congress Cataloging-in-Publication Data

Cooperman, Stephanie.
Wakeboarding: techniques and tricks / by Stephanie Cooperman.— 1st ed.
    p. cm. — (Rad sports)
Includes bibliographical references (p.) and index.
ISBN 0-8239-3850-6 (lib. bdg.)
1. Wakeboarding—Juvenile literature. [1. Wakeboarding.] I. Title.
II. Series.
GV840.W34 C66 2003
797.3'2—dc21

2002005045

Manufactured in the United States of America

CONTENTS

Introduction

Wakeboarding is one of the newest and most exciting radical, extreme sports. Wakeboarding is a combination of snowboarding and waterskiing. You ride a wakeboard by standing on it. It looks a lot like a snowboard, but it is longer and wider and has a rudder on the bottom to help turn on the water.

Don't worry, wakeboards have bindings so your feet don't slip off. As wakeboarders are towed behind motorboats at speeds of up to twenty miles per hour, you can do tricks such as flip, roll, grind, and spin. By using the boat's wake as a ramp, these boards can fly through the air and land safely on the water.

Sound easy? Well, it's not quite easy, but wakeboarding is fun to learn. You can even learn some cool-sounding tricks like the "roast beef" or the "back scratcher." You have to be safe to wakeboard properly, however. Having the right equipment helps. You also have to practice. Even getting up for the first time isn't as easy as it looks! Most important, you have to want to have fun.

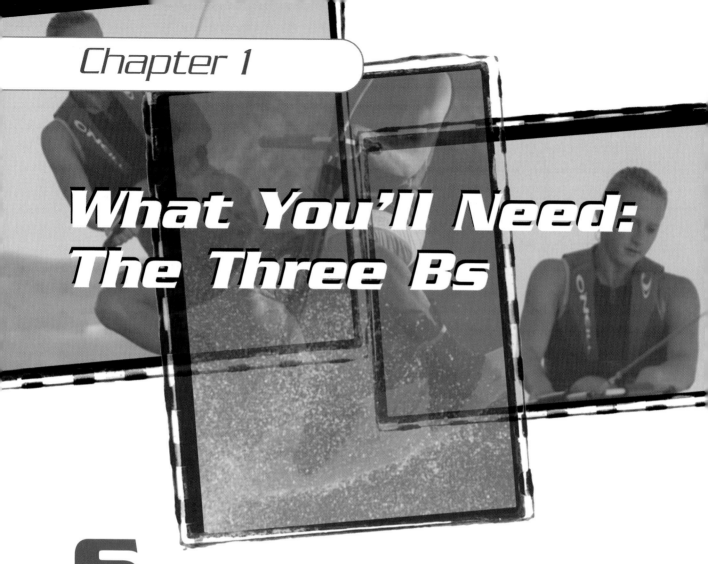

Chapter 1

What You'll Need: The Three Bs

Since you're ready to wakeboard, let's look at what you need to begin this water sport. Wakeboarders need access to a large body of water, a board on which to ride, and bindings to help stay on the board.

Getting a Boat

To wakeboard, you need the use of a boat. Luckily, what you don't need is a specially designed boat that you may have seen used on television for wakeboarding competitions. Just make sure the boat used can pull you out of the water and manage a speed of twenty miles per hour.

Creating a wake on which the wakeboard can be jumped or do tricks is key for any boat. Most boats can do this, but some are a little better than others. V-hull boats (boats in which the hull is shaped like a "V") cut through the water and make consistent wakes. Also, inboard/outboard (I/O) boats sit low in the water when going only twenty miles per hour. They do this because their heavy engines (more like a car engine changed for use to power a boat) sit in the rear and drag low in the water at slow speeds. I/Os can make big wakes—a foot or more—which help wakeboarders launch into the air as they speed over them.

Ask a Friend

Boats can be very expensive. Some can cost as much as $30,000! You don't need to buy a boat to be a wakeboarder. There are many places where you can rent a boat for a day. You can also borrow a friend's boat, or wakeboard with that friend. In fact, most people begin wakeboarding by going out on a friend's boat.

The History of the Sport

Wakeboarding started in 1985 when a surfer named Tony Finn created the skurfer. The skurfer looked like a small surfboard. This mini-surfboard wasn't used on rolling waves, however. Finn rode his skurfer on the back of a ski boat! The problem was that Finn hadn't made bindings for his board. It was very hard for him to stay up on a skurfer until two of Finn's wind-surfer buddies offered their help. They gave him the foot straps from their windsurfing boards. Wakeboarding was born!

Wakeboards are made in different sizes and widths to fit the various body sizes of the wakeboarders who ride them.

The Best Board for You

There are many styles and sizes of wakeboards from which to choose. When you first enter a ski shop, it's easy to get confused about which board is best for you. Don't be. Sales associates can help you out, and you should ask what the different kinds of boards can do for you on the water.

Most wakeboards are made of the same materials as water skis. A foam or polyurethane (plastic) core is covered by fiberglass or fiberglass/graphite composite (advanced and pro boards). Wakeboards are between 120 and 150 centimeters (47 to 59 inches) long. Their widths range from 39 to 43 centimeters (18.5 to 23 inches).

Wakeboards have one, two, or three fins on the bottom to help stability and turning ability. More fins equal a more stable board but cut down on trick maneuverability. The other factor affecting stability and steering is a board's rocker. The rocker is a board's curve on the bottom measured from front tip to back. Usually wakeboards have a rocker between 5 and 6 centimeters (less than 2 inches to just over 2 inches).

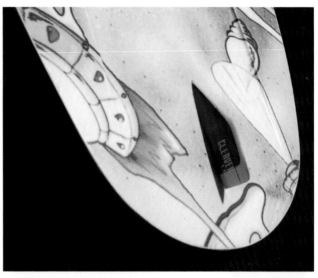

When choosing a board, remember that the most important factor is your weight. Purchasing a wakeboard that is too short for your body size will ruin your experience and be a waste of money. Generally, a person weighing up to 160 pounds should look for a board 125–135 cm (49–53 inches) long. Someone weighing 160–180 pounds should look for a board 135–140 cm (53–55 inches) long. And those weighing more than 180 should look for a board 140 cm (55 inches) long or longer.

Beginners should choose a twin-tipped board. Twin-tipped means both the nose and heel are sloped upward. This allows you to ski both forward and backward (fakie). When you begin doing tricks, a twin-tipped board will give you the best control.

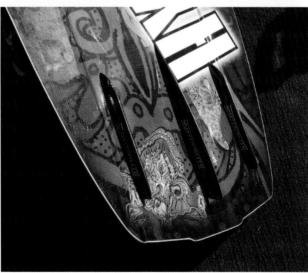

Wakeboards have tail fins (one, two, or three) that help boarders control and turn their boards. The number of fins determines how much control the boarder has.

Fitting Your Style

Wakeboarders are known for their outrageous personalities and even crazier styles. Let the colors and graphics on your board reflect who you are.

Whether it's wild patterns or fierce creatures that adorn your board, pick one out that fits your character. While you're cutting the wake, you want to show that you have the edge—on your board and with your moves.

Two types of bindings are available for wakeboards. These include strap bindings *(top)* and adjustable slip-on bindings *(bottom)*.

Bound Tight and Finned Out!

In order not to slip off the board, you're going to need bindings for your feet. Bungee bindings used to be the only ones available. These adjust to different foot sizes easily and are simple to get into. But bungee bindings don't give your feet a good hold. They can be used for recreational wakeboarding and to teach people how to get up and maneuver. Bungee bindings will not hold you in, however, when you want to do tricks.

10

Parks Bonifay

The boarder everyone calls "Wonderboy" blows the competition out of the water. Twenty-one-year-old Parks Bonifay is consistently ranked number one in the world. It's no wonder! He started wakeboarding at age twelve. He is even in the *Guinness Book of World Records* for being the youngest waterskier ever—he first skied at just six months and twenty-nine days old!

If you're going to do tricks, you want to get a boot binding. They are made in different sizes to best fit your foot. Most are adjustable so that others can use the board, too. Usually you can adjust certain areas of the binding so it conforms to your foot. Bindings are made to be safe. They work similarly to water-ski boot bindings. When you fall, your body weight will usually pull you right out of the boot.

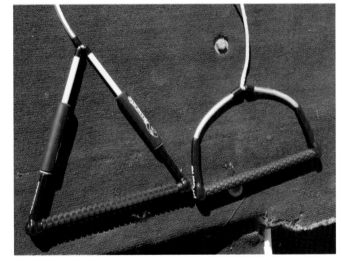

You Can Handle It!

Of course, you'll need a handle and towrope so the boat can pull you in the water. Wakeboard rope handles are wider than water-ski

A wakeboard ski rope handle *(left)* is wider than the handle used by water-skiers *(right)*. Wakeboarders need a wider handle to do tricks, such as passing the handle behind their backs.

rope handles (13–15 inches wide, or 33–38 centimeters, as opposed to 11–12 inches, or 28–30.5 centimeters, wide). The longer handle allows you to hold on more easily while you move during tricks. When you swing the handle behind your back or do other handle-passing tricks, you'll feel more in control.

Wakeboard towropes come as low-stretch or no-stretch, and they should be between 60 and 70 feet (18–21 meters) long. The shorter the rope is, the higher and longer you can jump off the wake. Low-stretch ropes are made of polyethylene plastic. Under normal wakeboarding stress, this rope will stretch only 1 percent of total length. No-stretch ropes are made of Spectra, a synthetic material that allows less than half of 1 percent of total length stretch.

Adding weight to the boat using fat sacks filled with water pushes the boat down into the water, which helps make a larger wake.

Enhancing Your Wake

There are lots of other gadgets you can get to fine-tune your style. Fat sacks are water-filled bags that help weigh the boat in the water to create a bigger wake. Pylons and tuna towers are tall poles that—like shorter ropes—allow you to get more air. But beginners don't require any of this other gear. It can be very expensive. It's better to go with the necessities and then buy add-ons once you've mastered the basics. Start simple.

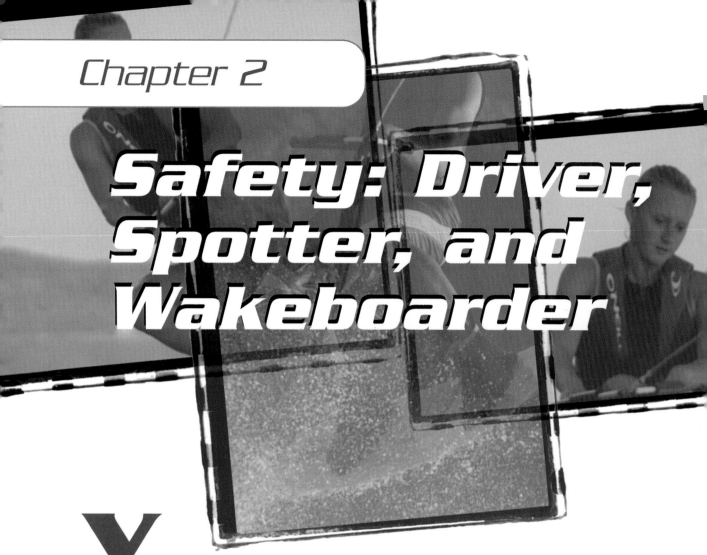

Chapter 2

Safety: Driver, Spotter, and Wakeboarder

You may feel like you're flying solo when you're zooming across the water. In some ways you are, but your transportation—the boat—is piloted and also carries a spotter. Boating laws and water safety rules apply to wakeboarders and those in the boat. Before you land your first trick, you need to know safety rules and boating laws.

In the Boat . . .

There must be at least two people in the boat when a wakeboarder is in the water. One person is the driver, and the other is the spotter. Most states today require boat drivers to have a license. As with automobile licenses, many states require boaters to be at least sixteen years old to earn a boating license. You should find out which laws apply to your state.

The driver *(left)* must face forward at all times and watch the direction of the boat's progress. The spotter *(right)* needs to watch the wakeboarder to tell the driver when the boarder has fallen.

The other person in the boat is called the spotter. While the driver watches the water ahead, the spotter watches the wakeboarder. The spotter's main job is to tell the driver when the wakeboarder has fallen or let go of the rope. A firm "Down!" shouted above the roar of the engine is sufficient to signal the driver.

The wakeboarder should use verbal communication when telling the spotter when he or she is ready to get up. Shouting "Hit it!" is clear enough. The spotter also relays hand signals passed to him or her by the wakeboarder.

Now what does the wakeboarder need to tell the driver? Several things, actually. Wakeboarders often want to travel at a certain speed or are tired and ready to drop the rope. Each of these actions can be signaled to the spotter so there's no confusion. After all, no one in the boat is going to hear screams from the wakeboarder. With a few simple hand signs, wakeboarders can let the spotter know what's up.

An outstretched palm beneath the chin: Means you're ready to stop

Thumbs up: Means speed up

Thumbs down: Means slow down

Before taking off, practice your hand signs with the spotter. He or she should be able to see and understand your signals before you get in the water. You don't want to show the spotter an outstretched palm and have the driver speed up!

The spotter relays hand signals from the wakeboarder to the driver: (1) Thumbs up means "Speed up the boat," (2) thumbs down means "Slow down," and (3) a flat palm held below the chin means "I'm ready to stop."

Your spotter will always be looking out for your signs as you wakeboard. If you feel you're losing control at any time, just give the thumbs down sign and the spotter will tell the driver to slow down. Really in trouble? Put your palm down and fingers below your chin to show that you want to stop. It's hard to keep your balance if your towrope isn't pulled tight. So when you're on the go, the driver should keep the boat's speed steady. Lean back to load the rope—or create tension—and you're ready to start movin'.

Your driver should not let the boat's speed exceed twenty miles per hour. Going faster won't make you a better wakeboarder. Even the professionals

Words to Wake By

All sports have jargon used for quick communication and recognition. Wakeboarding is no exception.

Left Foot Forward/Right Foot Forward

This is the foot closest to the boat.

Toeside/Frontside

Describes your toes or chest facing the wake when you do a trick.

Heelside/Backside

Describes your heels or back facing the wake when you do a trick.

Leading Edge

The side of the wakeboard that is closest to the boat.

Load the Line

To increase tension on the line as you approach the wake.

Trailing Edge

The side of the wakeboard that is farthest from the boat.

know that! Pick a speed that's comfortable for you. Also check your wakeboard. Most wakeboards come with instructions for a top speed. Anything faster than that and your wakeboard won't handle as well.

. . . And in the Water

The most important item you can wear while wakeboarding isn't that stylin' new pair of board shorts you just picked up. It's not even those cool shades. It's the life jacket you can't forget to put on. And not just any life jacket— one that is approved by the United States Coast Guard. Many states require them. All wakeboard competitors wear them. USCG-approved life jackets can save your life in the event of a bad wipeout. If you hit your head hard, you can be knocked unconscious. It's essential that you wear a life jacket.

Don't be scared of falling. It happens to everyone. Falling is part of learning the sport and will happen when you throw tricks. It's important not to panic when you fall. Most likely, your bindings will have released from the board. So you shouldn't be stuck in an awkward position. When you feel yourself about to fall or wipe out, tuck your body into a ball and let your momentum carry you into the water. You'll roll across the water a bit but then stop. No problem. Just locate your board and the boat. Your spotter will see you and direct the driver to stop and come get you. And, thanks to your life jacket, you'll be safe while you wait for your next tow.

A life jacket is designed to hold your head above water. Make sure the jacket fits snugly across the chest and over the shoulders.

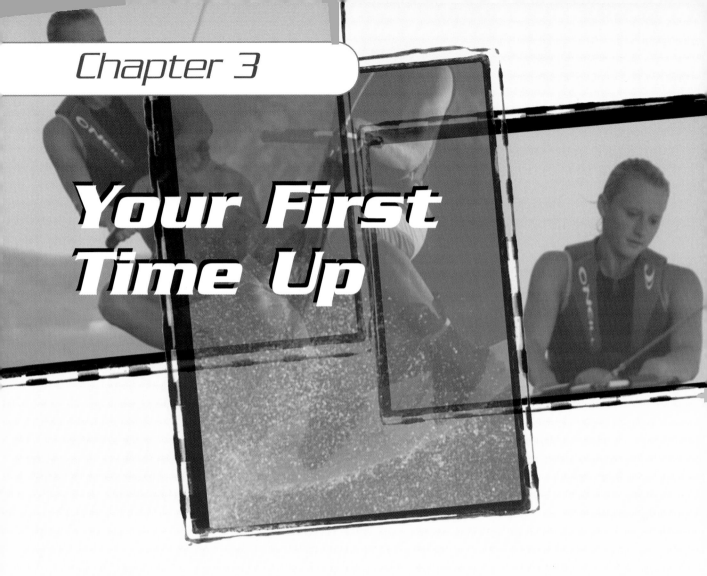

Chapter 3

Your First Time Up

Riding a wakeboard is done with a staggered stance—one foot in front of the other. But which foot should be at the front of your wakeboard? That's a question only you can answer. There is no right or wrong stance. You want to find which foot feels more comfortable in the front position. If you wakeboard with your left foot forward, you are a regular-footed rider. If you wakeboard with your right foot forward, you are a goofy-footed rider. Try each stance to see which feels more comfortable. Still can't decide? If you skateboard or snowboard, you probably want to go with the same foot forward for wakeboarding.

Getting Up

The boat driver will now move the boat forward until the rope becomes taut. When you're ready, yell "Hit it!"

Starting Position

Once you've got your feet in the boots, gently slide yourself into the water. Your spotter should hand or throw you the rope. Now you're ready to set your body in position. Place your palms down about shoulder-width apart on the handle. Bend your knees so that your wakeboard is on its side (frontside, with your toes pointing forward) in front of you. Keep your eyes straight ahead. The boat will pick up speed and your wakeboard will plow against the water. Now bring your knees up close to your chest and your hands just in front of your knees. Now you're in the starting position.

1. Keep your eyes straight ahead. The boat will pick up speed and your wakeboard will plow against the water.

2. Keep your hands tight on the handle and your arms set against your body's drag in the water.

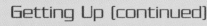

3 Getting Up (continued)

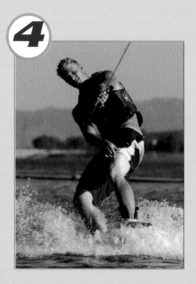

3. Use your feet to keep the plane (angle) of the board up. This will help the speed and water force the board to the surface, and you will rise with it. When you first come out of the water, you'll be in a squatting position.

4. As the wakeboard planes off (rides flat on top of the water) and stabilizes, turn the board forward and stand up. Keep your knees bent slightly and hold your arms out before you at chest height.

Getting up may take you a few tries. If you have ever water-skied, you'll find that getting up on a wakeboard is almost as easy, just a bit different because of your body position. There are a few common mistakes beginners make. If your wakeboard keeps darting out in front of you, you probably find yourself landing on your butt. Either you're not bending your knees enough or you're pulling on the handle too much. Both these problems are a matter of balance. Don't rely on pulling on the rope, as this will usually make you sit or lean back. Instead, let the boat do the pulling and find your balance position over your legs and atop the board.

Body Position

Your body position is crucial in wakeboarding. Keep your upper body—that's everything above your waist—facing the boat. This part of your body doesn't even have to move while you're boarding. Your shoulders should be square to the back of the boat as you ride. Most important, always have an eye on where your handle is. When you are going straight, keep the handle low—near your body's center of gravity. You'll have to move the handle to do lots of tricks. But if the handle is a little above and in front of your forward hip, it'll be easy to move when the time is right. If you keep the handle closer to your chest or if it sinks to your knees, your balance will be thrown off. And you'll probably topple over. The closer the handle is to your waist, the better control you will have.

Moving Inside the Wake

Heelside and toeside pressure, and a little body lean, are what get you moving side to side. Practice these steps to move inside the wake.

1. Apply pressure to your heels and lean into the turn. Now you're moving in the heelside direction.

2 Moving Inside the Wake
[continued]

2. Ease off the pressure and straighten your body. Your heel-side momentum will stop.

3. Now apply pressure to your toes and lean into that turn. You can feel yourself moving toeside against the tension of the pulling boat.

Turning from one side to the other is a matter of feel, so take your time and find how your balance affects your turning performance. Remember to always be mindful of your body position and where your handle is. And always look in the direction you're going—not where you've just been. Soon this heelside-then-toeside motion will become natural. It'll be almost as easy as walking.

Moving Over and Outside the Wake

After you've learned to comfortably turn back and forth behind the boat inside the wake, it's time to cross the wake. Crossing the wake is key to putting the basic skills of the sport together. Master these skills before you try any tricks.

Going over the wake, and then across both wakes, is all about riding over the bump without losing balance or catching an edge and going head first into the water. It's easiest to start crossing the wake on your toeside if you are regular footed, or heelside if you're goofy footed.

1. For regular-footed skiers, put pressure on your toes so that you are moving across the water. Increase the pressure as you move to the wake.

2. Flex your legs and ride over the bump of the wake. Make sure the rope tension is high to help set your balance over the wake. There, you've done it!

3. When you cut the wake, keep going until you are 10 to 15 feet (3 to 4.5 meters) outside the wake.

The key to learning how to go across the wake is gradually increasing the pressure on your toes (or heels) as you move to the outside. You don't want to go slow over the wake, where it can throw off your balance or make you dip the wakeboard's nose into the water and catch the toe for a face plant. Keep your knees bent and your eyes on the horizon in the direction you're moving.

Goofy or Regular?

Here's another exercise you can do to find out which foot should go in the front boot: Stand with your feet shoulder-width apart. Have a friend stand behind you. Your friend should push you gently from behind. You're going to reach one leg out to stop yourself from falling over. The foot that doesn't move should be your forward foot.

Cutting into the Wake

1. From a position 10 to 15 feet (3 to 4.5 meters) behind the boat, begin putting pressure on your toes.

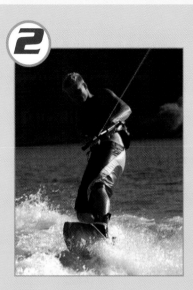

2. Move toward the wake toeside with the rope tight, your knees bent, and the handle at your front hip. Gradually increase pressure and gain speed.

3. Flex your legs as you cross the wake toeside and slow down so you face forward behind the boat again. There, you've done it.

Crossing the wake is the first step to doing really awesome tricks. This technique is essential to learning most moves. Getting your balance and keeping your legs under you takes practice. Don't feel you have to prove yourself, but don't hold back your desire for speed. You'll fall, you'll catch an edge, you'll fly face first into the white froth behind the boat. Don't worry, though, that's what it takes to learn sometimes. Practice cutting across the wake until you can do it many times—without falling. Only when you have the basics down will you be able to get some big air.

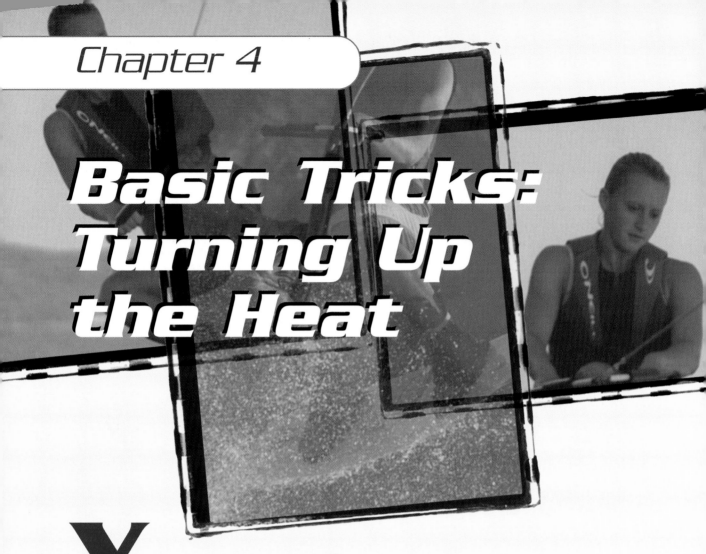

Chapter 4

Basic Tricks: Turning Up the Heat

You may be surprised to learn that crossing the wake by putting pressure on your heels or your toes—called edging—was your first trick. And you thought you didn't know anything yet! You'll probably find that heelside edging is easier than toeside edging. This is because it's more natural for you to lean back on your heels. But practice crossing the wake on both edges. You'll need both techniques to do many tricks, including the basic tricks on the following pages.

Bunny Hop

Want to jump a little? Now is your chance. The bunny hop is a great jump for beginners. Remember to load your rope by pulling on it and pressing back on your board at the same time. This creates tension and force that helps you gain speed when you cut outside the wake. You need this tension to properly gain momentum for the bunny hop.

1. Cut to the outside of the wake heelside. Flatten out by shifting your weight to your toes.

2. Ease up on the rope at the same time. Now push the board with your heels into the water and quickly push away with your toes. This releases the tension between you, the rope, and the water. You should pop into the air.

3. When you land, keep your knees bent, your eyes toward the boat, and the handle at your front hip.

It's just as easy to do a bunny hop on your toeside. Simply cut out on your toeside the same way you did on your heelside. Push your board into the water with your toes. Then push away with your heels. And you're in the air again!

The Wake Side Slide

This is a fun trick that lets you ride on the wakeboard's side with both feet pointing forward. Learning to side slide gets you ready to pivot on the water to ski fakie (sometimes called switch).

1. Ride onto the top of the wake and get ready to quickly pivot your board toeside.

2. Pivot the board quickly toeside so your feet are pointing forward (open stance). Make sure as you pivot that you pitch the board back so that the board side will ride above the water. If you pitch the board forward, it will bite the water and you'll trip.

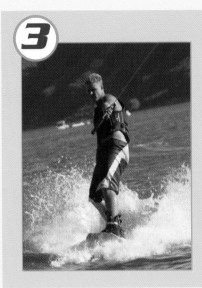

3. To return to the forward position, shift your weight to the back of the board. Let the back fin catch the water and it will pull the board around. Now the front of your board is pointing forward again.

The board slide is done atop the wake so that the board's front and back fins come out of the water. This lets the board easily slide on its side without catching or tripping the rider.

Riding Fakie

Changing to the fakie, or switchstance, position—with your opposite foot forward—is another good trick to learn when you're just starting out. You'll have to switch to fakie to do many advanced tricks. To start, give the spotter the thumbs down sign so the driver knows to slow down. The boat should slow down enough to make the water "mushy," or soft under your wakeboard.

1. Keep the handle near your back hip and ride on top of the wake.

Riding Fakie (continued)

2. Now pivot as if you're doing a board slide. Keep the pivot moving 180 degrees until the board is in the fakie (backward) position.

3. The foot that was in the back should now be in the front. Give the thumbs up sign and off you go—riding fakie!

If you shift your weight forward as you pivot past the board slide position, the front fin will catch the water and help you complete the 180-degree turn to fakie.

Bunny Hop 180

The bunny hop 180 is an easy trick that gets you riding fakie with a little jump and pivot. You begin in your normal stance and wind up in the fakie position after the jump.

The same rules apply for toeside jumps. Approach the wake by putting pressure on your toes. Bring the handle to your front hip while you're in the air. With toeside jumps, the trick is not to lean forward too much. Just look at the direction you want to go and don't move your upper body.

1. Start outside the wake heel-side. Load your rope and shift your weight on your heels to begin your bunny hop.

2. As you shift your weight on your toes and spring into the air, turn your back hip toward the handle. Pivot your board while in the air.

3. As you land you should be riding fakie (backward). Don't worry if you haven't completed your pivot. You'll ride on your side for a moment until the back fin catches and pulls your tip around fakie.

Jumping

Jumping over the wake is almost as easy as boarding over it. Jumping across the wake is what wakeboarding is all about, too! Getting up in the air, flying across the wake, and landing on the downside of the opposite wake takes finesse and balance.

1. For a heelside jump (and most other jumps), start about 15 feet (4.5 meters) outside the wake. Cut hard on your heels to gain speed as you approach the wake. Keep your knees bent. As you come to the wake ease up to give yourself time to set up the jump.

2. As the board goes up and over the wake, push off to launch into the air. You should make your push at the wake crest (top). Keep your knees bent and your arms down. Stay over the top of the board.

3. Come down with your weight over the board and legs flexed to absorb the landing.

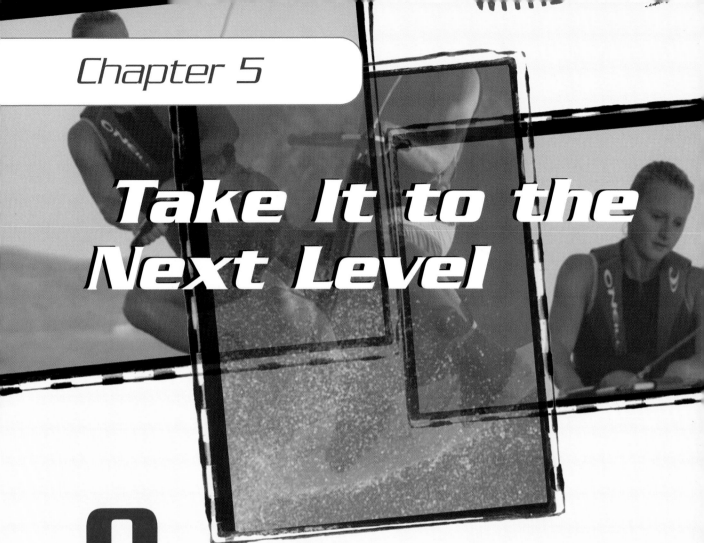

Chapter 5

Take It to the Next Level

Once you have the basics down and can easily board slide, ride fakie, and jump, it's time for some more difficult tricks. Doing tricks while in the air is where you want to take your wakeboarding skills. The excitement of flying through the air and grabbing the board or kicking it back gives you as much freedom as anyone could ever want.

Back Scratcher

For a little excitement, the back scratcher teaches you to move your body in the air without losing your balance. It's a variation on the wake jump. Keeping your balance, or air position, is important for all wakeboard tricks. You must be able to feel comfortable in the air to do the basic tricks in this book.

1. Cut heelside to the wake from 15 feet (4.5 meters) out. Launch in the air as high as possible.

2. At the highest point in the air, pull your legs up behind you. Try to touch your back with the board.

3. As you start to drop, bring your legs down and flex your knees to absorb the landing.

Tip Grab

Grabs are another variation on jumping. There are several types of grabs in which you use one hand to grab different parts of the board while in the air. The tip grab is a good starting point.

1. Cut heelside to the wake from 15 feet (4.5 meters) out. Ease up at the wake and launch as high as you can.

2. Launch with the board tip angled up. Bend your legs up toward your waist and grab the tip of the board (use whatever hand works best).

3. Release the board as you come down. Flex your legs to absorb the landing.

The trick to grabbing is not to bend down to your board. Bring your knees to your chest instead.

Roast Beef

The roast beef takes a little more time to perform in the air because you have to bring the entire board up to your hand. Keep your strong hand on the rope so you stay connected to the boat while in the air.

1. Cut heelside to the wake from 15 feet (4.5 meters) out. Ease up at the wake and launch as high as you can.

2. As you rise to your highest point, bend your knees up to your waist. Reach down between your legs toeside and grab the board. Hold this position as long as possible. Your friends will be awed!

3. As you come down, release the board and keep your knees and ankles flexed for the landing.

Tail Grab

For a final grab, we've chosen the tail grab so that you can show off the three basic grab positions: front, middle, and tail.

1. Cut heelside to the wake from 15 feet (4.5 meters) out. Hit the wake with speed and launch as high as you can.

2. Level your board out quickly and bring your knees up. Reach back and grab the tail. (If you want, extend your front leg to look really cool.)

3. On your way down, let go of the tail, extend your legs, and flex your knees when you hit the water to absorb the landing.

The Twister

The twister is not a grab. It gets your upper and lower body moving in opposite directions in the air. Try to get big air to make this trick look really rad!

1. Cut heelside to the wake and launch as high as you can.

2. Once in the air, twist your upper body toward the boat (this is the easiest way to get good movement) and your lower body away from the boat. Hold this position until you start to drop.

3. Set up your landing by twisting back and flexing your knees. Absorb the landing and get ready for another trick!

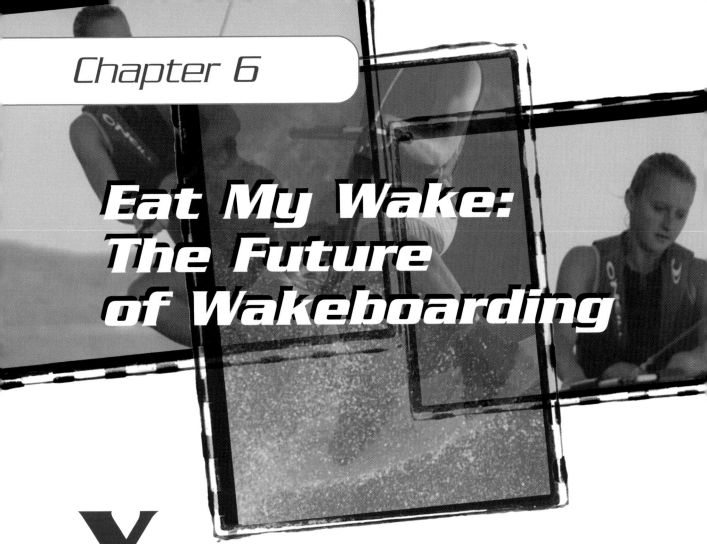

Chapter 6

Eat My Wake: The Future of Wakeboarding

You've got enough knowledge about wakeboarding now to get you started. For unlimited practice and advice from the experts, consider going to a wakeboarding camp or school. They are all over the country, so wherever you live there's probably one near enough to make it worth the trip. A summer wake school program will give instruction from experts. These people were once beginners like you, so keep your eyes and ears open.

Ready to Compete

So you've practiced your tricks. You've gone to wakeboarding camp. Maybe you've even thought of some of your own original tricks. Maybe it's time for you to compete. If you want to try your tricks in competition, you need to do your homework.

Since you'll be starting on the amateur level, look for beginner competitions. The World Wakeboard Association (WWA) can help you find a competition that is close to where you live. Amateur events are open to boarders of all levels. It's a good place to learn from other beginners and show off what you've got.

Each event is different. Besides the in-the-water competition, some events feature skill workshops where you can get tips and advice from professional boarders. Others have booths where you can test out the newest gear from boards to bindings. Still others have great music and even better food. Whatever competition you go to, you can be sure there's going to be lots of people who love the same sport that you do.

When you compete, you'll be judged in two different events: freestyle and expression. During the freestyle event, you pick the tricks you're going to try during your run. Depending on which tricks you pick, you'll be put in a category—beginner, intermediate, or advanced. Once you're in the water, you'll be judged on how many of your tricks you complete and how good your style is.

In the expression session, you'll have a few minutes to do whatever you want in the water. This is when you can get creative. You'll be judged on the difficulty of your tricks, your style, and your aggressiveness. The expression session is the best time to let the best that you do hang out there for all to see. Do tricks back to back, combine tricks, grab huge air!

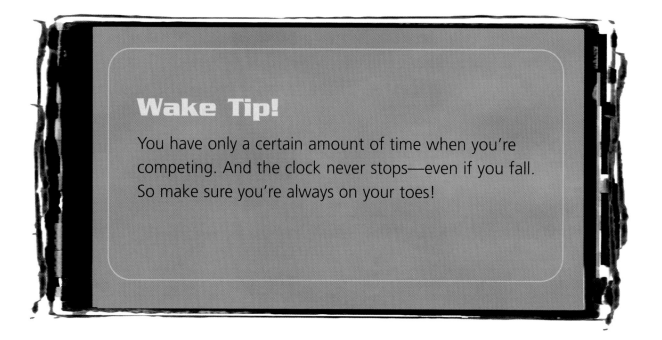

Wake Tip!

You have only a certain amount of time when you're competing. And the clock never stops—even if you fall. So make sure you're always on your toes!

Professional wakeboarders compete nearly year-round. They can also practice several hours each day. This is why, when you see them on television, they make the tricks they do look effortless.

The Real Deal

Professional competitions are great places to watch and learn. Professional wakeboarders are sponsored by sports equipment companies. They compete for cash prizes. Judges score professionals based on the difficulty of their tricks, their style, and how much air they get before they land. Sound pretty intimidating? It shouldn't. Just watch and learn. These men and women who were once just starting out like you.

Professionals are given a rank in the World Cup—the combined results from fifteen different tournaments. This is how the best male and female wakeboarders in the world are determined. One of these tournaments is the X Games. They're like the Olympics for extreme sports. Boarders flip, twist, grind, and grab in front of huge audiences and television cameras.

What's next for boarders on the professional circuit? Rumor has it wakeboarding could be added to the Olympics very soon. The 2004 Olympic Games in Athens, Greece, will showcase waterskiing for the first time. It's only a matter of time before wakeboarders compete for their very own medals and glory!

Practice, Practice, Practice!

So you think you have what it takes to be a wakeboarder? Determination. Perseverance. The will to get up even when you fall. These are all attributes of wakeboarders today. Wakeboarding is now the fastest growing water sport in the world, so it's a great time to take part. Learning the best tricks and the wildest style takes practice—and lots of it.

Glossary

bindings The straps or boots that keep a boarder's feet firmly on the board.

driver The experienced person driving the boat that pulls the wakeboarder.

edge The side of your board (noun), or leaning on one side of the board (verb).

fakie/switchstance Riding the board backward.

fat sacks Large, water-filled bags put in the boat that weigh the boat down to help make a bigger wake.

fins Pieces that attach to the bottom of the board to help make it turn.

goofy footed Riding a wakeboard right foot forward.

handle What a wakeboarder holds on to as the boat pulls him or her.

life jacket An inflatable vest that keeps a person's head above water.

load the rope Creating tension on the towrope to prepare for a trick.

outboard A type of boat where the engine hangs off the back of the boat.

pylons Tall poles in a boat on which the rope is mounted for wakeboarding that give the boarder more upward pull.

regular footed Riding a wakeboard left foot forward.

skurfer An earlier version of the wakeboard that did not have bindings.

spotter The person in the boat responsible for watching the wakeboarder and communicating his or her hand signals to the driver.

towrope The rope connected to the boat that a wakeboarder uses to board.

wake The trail the boat leaves behind.

For More Information

World Wakeboard Association (WWA)

P.O. Box 1964
Auburndale, FL 33823
(863) 551-1683
Web site: http://www.thewwa.com

Videos

Skurf's Up. FLF Films, 1999.
Switch. Sidewayz Films, 1999.
Wakeboarding Made Easy 2.1 with Troy Navarro. Inks Production
    Company, 2001.
Wide Awake. Liquid Force Films, 2000.

Web Sites

Due to the changing nature of Internet links, the Rosen Publishing Group,
Inc., has developed an online list of Web sites related to the subject of this
book. This site is updated regularly. Please use this link to access the list:

http://www.rosenlinks.com/rs/watt/

For Further Reading

Eck, Kristin. *Wakeboarding: Check It Out!* New York: Powerkids Press, 2001.

Hayhurst, Chris. *Wakeboarding! Throw a Tantrum*. New York: The Rosen Publishing Group, Inc., 2000.

McKenna, Anne T. *Extreme Wakeboarding*. Mankato, MN: Capstone Press, 2000.

Magazines

Wake Boarding
330 West Canton Avenue
Winter Park, FL 32792
(407) 628-4802
http://www.wakeboardingmag.com

Bibliography

Gravity Games Homepage. *"Wakeboarding History."* Retrieved March 12, 2002 (http://www.gravitygames.com).

Hayhurst, Chris. *Wakeboarding! Throw a Tantrum*. New York: The Rosen Publishing Group, Inc., 2000.

Ladyboarder.com. "Tricks." Retrieved March 16, 2002 (http://www.ladyboarder.com).

McKenna, Anne T. *Extreme Wakeboarding.* Mankato, MN: Capstone Press, 2000.

Wakeworld.com. "Board Guide." Retrieved March 6, 2002 (http://www.wakeworld.com).

Weber, Jason. *Wakeboarding on the Edge*. Mays Landing, NJ: Sports on the Edge, 2000.

Index

About the Author

Stephanie Cooperman, a graduate of the University of Pennsylvania, is currently employed at a large book publishing company. She is a writer who freelances for both print and Web site materials. She loves water sports and has practiced the tricks mentioned in this book in her living room—much to the chagrin of her roommates. She lives in New York City.

Acknowledgments

Thanks to Chris Williams, Katie Lorier, Laurie Schakett, Perry Richmond, and to Brett Tilly of Tilly's Marine.

Credits

Cover, pp. 8–12, 14, 15, 17, 19–25, 27–32, 34–38 © Tony Donaldson/Icon SMI/Rosen Publishing; pp. 4–5 © Neil Rabinowitz/Corbis; p. 41 © AP/Wide World Photos.

Editor

Mark Beyer

Design and Layout

Les Kanturek